A KID'S GUIDE TO

San Francisco

Photography by Sandra Cannon

Written by Sara Day

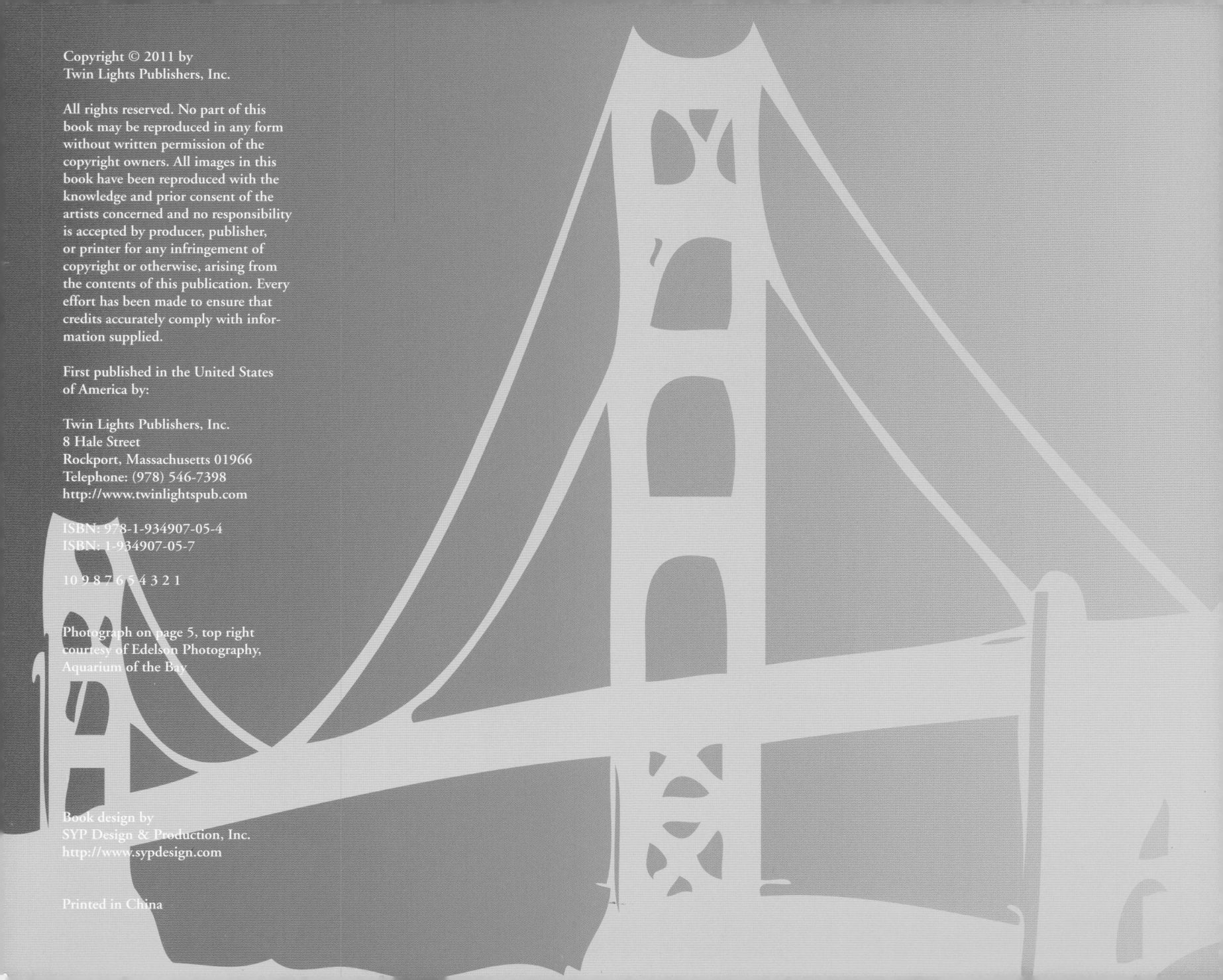

First published in the United States
of America by:

Twin Lights Publishers, Inc.
8 Hale Street
Rockport, Massachusetts 01966
Telephone: (978) 546-7398
http://www.twinlightspub.com

ISBN: 978-1-934907-05-4
ISBN: 1-934907-05-7

10 9 8 7 6 5 4 3 2 1

Photograph on page 5, top right
courtesy of Edelson Photography,
Aquarium of the Bay

Book design by
SYP Design & Production, Inc.
http://www.sypdesign.com

Printed in China

Welcome to Yerba Buena! That's what San Francisco used to be called until the United Sates took it over way back in 1847. That's just one of a bucketful of cool things to find out about one of the most exciting and kid-friendly cities in the country.

This book can be your own personal tour guide as you venture up and down hills to explore dozens of interesting landmarks all over the city—from the incredibly awesome Golden Gate Bridge, to the gingerbread-style Painted Ladies, Fisherman's Wharf, and crazy twisted Lombard Street.

There's so much to discover here in the "City by the Bay." *A Kid's Guide to San Francisco* makes it easy, with over 100 fun and interesting facts from Alcatraz to the San Francisco Zoo. Check out Ghirardelli Chocolate Factory, tour a submarine, learn about the Pony Express, or discover an ancient redwood forest—San Francisco is the place to be for things to do and see.

Our user-friendly, A to Z format covers a little bit of everything including: history, art, culture, music, sports and more. It's easy to read and is illustrated with tons of beautiful color photos of famous buildings, parks, and landmarks you'll come to recognize.

Keep tabs on all the great things you see and do with the trip guide at the back of the book. There's even a fun "Been There Done That!" sticker map that'll come in handy when keeping track of some of your most favorite landmarks.

Whether you're riding the rolling hills on a classic San Francisco cable car, racing along on the super-modern BART transit system, or hiking along the scenic Bay Trail, this guide is packed with fun facts that'll give you the lowdown on one of the most exciting cities on the planet.

city incorporated:
April 15th, 1850

area:
46.69 square miles

estimated population:
815,358

Alcatraz Island
The Rock

High atop a small, rocky island out in the middle of San Francisco Bay, sits a building that used to be one of the toughest prisons in America. Cold, damp, and downright unfriendly, Alcatraz was home to some of the most notorious bad guys around, including Al Capone and George "Machine Gun" Kelly. It used to be a military fort before it was a prison. If you decide to take a tour, just remember, they say that no one has ever successfully escaped from Alcatraz!

Angel Island
The Western Gateway to America

One of the most beautiful island parks in America is only a brisk ferry ride away. Hike to the highest point on the island, Mount Livermore, and get ready to be blown away by the perfect panoramic view. On a clear day, you can see all five Bay Area bridges. Angel Island is known as "The Ellis Island of the West," because it was here that hundreds of thousands of immigrants, mostly Asian, made their way to America way back in 1910. At Immigration Station you can still see the poems of hope they carved into the walls.

Antisubmarine Net
Gotcha!

During World War II, San Francisco had some pretty clever ways to protect the bay. One idea was an enormous underwater net that stretched clear across the bay. It was the third line of defense behind huge, powerful guns and a minefield scattered with about 600 mines.

Aquarium of the Bay
Discover an Underwater Paradise

Mysterious and awe-inspiring life thrives just beneath the waves of San Francisco Bay, the largest estuary on the west coast. You can feed a Bat Ray, and touch Skates, Leopard Sharks, and Sea Stars at the *Touch the Bay* exhibit. This totally amazing exhibit has cool tunnels that give you a chance to scuba dive without getting hypothermia! The Aquarium of the Bay is a marine nature center dedicated to the conservation of San Francisco Bay and all marine environments.

Aquatic Park Lagoon
Chilly Thrills!

Just behind the Maritime Museum is San Francisco's favorite swimming hole. Whether you're just splashing around with your family or training for a serious open-water swim meet, this pretty lagoon's water temperature averages between 50 and 60 degrees. *Brrr!* Don't forget the hot chocolate!

Asian Art Museum

Travel back in time through 6,000 years of history at one of the biggest Asian art museums in the world. With over 17,000 works of art, this museum's collection was so huge, they had to move it from Golden Gate Park to a larger building at the Civic Center. Art, films, demonstrations, and exciting programs are just some of the ways you can discover amazing Asian culture.

Balclutha Clipper Ship

Just over 300 feet long, with the tallest of three masts measuring 145 feet high, this spectacular 19th-century classic is one big boat! Built in 1886, *Balclutha* has had a long career carrying cargo all over the world. Also known as "Star of Alaska" and "Pacific Queen," she is the last square-rigged ship in San Francisco Bay. Moored in Maritime National Historic Park, today *Balclutha* is a living museum waiting to welcome you aboard.

Bandshell
There's Music in the Air!

Come and enjoy a Sunday afternoon band concert at Spreckels Temple of Music, also known as the "bandshell." Built in 1900, it was a gift from Claus Spreckels, a man who was in the sugar business. Sweet deal for the city! The bandshell was damaged by two earthquakes, one in 1906 and one in 1989. It was repaired with special reinforcements made just for earthquakes and reopened in 1994.

Bank of Canton
Can You Hear Me Now?

The Bank of Canton in Chinatown used to be called the Chinese Telephone Exchange. First ringing up customers in 1894, it was Chinatown's first public telephone station and had a small switchboard where operators knew each customer by name, not by number.

Barbary Coast Trail
Get Your Walking Shoes On!

When you see this bronze medallion along the sidewalk, you'll know you're on the Barbary Coast Trail. Just follow the arrows to see some important historic sites along the 3.8-mile walking tour. From Union Square to Nob Hill, from the Gold Rush to the 1906 earthquake, walking this trail is an adventure. And, if you get hungry, don't worry, there are lots of great places to chow down along the way!

BART
One Cool Ride

The Bay Area Rapid Transit system, better known as BART, is famous for being the most luxurious public transportation system around. The sleek, 70-foot-long trains run along 104 miles of track and link 43 stations in style with carpeting, air conditioning, and fancy lighting. You can travel underwater on BART because it runs under the bay through one of the longest underwater transit tubes in the world. BART opened in 1972, and the trains still have a very modern design.

Bay Area Discovery Museum
A Mind Blast for Kids!

The Bay Area Discovery Museum is a great place for kids to learn and play. Inside and out, they can explore and create with hands-on science and environmental exhibits, special events, festivals and more. It's 7.5 acres of pure fun, so get curious, get creative, and get going!

Bay Bridge
The Other Way Across

The Bay Bridge connects the cities of San Francisco and Oakland and is actually made up of six different parts that span 8.4 miles. The central part of the bridge is, in fact, a 76-foot-wide bore tunnel that goes right through Yerba Buena Island. The original Bay Bridge was built in 1936 using 18,500 tons of wire, 1 million cubic yards of concrete, and 200,000 gallons of paint!

Bell-ringing Champs

Some of San Francisco's best cable car bell-ringers have been chiming in every year since 1949 when the first bell-ringing contest took place. Since then, people gather in Union Square every June for the annual event of choosing the "king of ding-a-ling," and to celebrate the history of these unique cable cars. Can you believe that in 1947, San Francisco cable cars were almost replaced with plain old buses?

Bison Paddock
Big Beasts in a Big City

What's a heard of Bison doing in a big city? They're part of the San Francisco Zoo. The Bison Paddock is a large area in Golden Gate Park where these big, hairy animals roam. Amazingly, the herd we see today was brought from Wyoming over 25 years ago.

Blue Angels
Catch'em if You Can!

Flying high, the famous Blue Angels tear across the skyline during an awesome air show that's all part of Fleet Week in San Francisco. Flown by the most skilled pilots in the world, these powerful fighter jets are MEGA-LOUD and will shake you to the core!

Blue Jeans

Ever wonder where blue jeans came from? Well, the first denim jeans originated right here in San Francisco back in 1873 by Jacob Davis and Levi Strauss. But, back then they were made for hard work, not fashion.

Buena Vista Park
Head for the Hills!

This 589-foot slope was first called (can you guess?)—Hill Park! It was the first park in San Francisco's park system. In 1906, it became the prime spot for people to watch the fires in the city below that were caused by the Great Earthquake of 1906. Today, the 36-acre area is a beautiful park that features a magnificent forest of huge trees, paved trails, and playgrounds.

Cable Cars
San Francisco's Most Famous Ride

When Andrew Hallidie noticed how tough it was for heavy, horse-drawn streetcars to make it up and down San Francisco's steep hills, he came up with the idea to use wire ropes to pull cable cars along tracks. In 1873, he tested the first cable car system at Nob Hill. It was a success, much to the relief of a lot of tired feet (and hooves, too!).

At the Cable Car Museum, you can see a collection of old-time cable cars and check out the mechanical displays with huge engines and spinning wheels to see how it all worked.

California Academy of Sciences

How does a star form? Where did all the dinosaurs go? How are coral reefs 'alive'? You can find the answers to these and more at the incredible California Academy of Sciences. It's unlike any other natural history museum in the world. The brand new, multi-million dollar facility is an aquarium, planetarium, natural history museum, a 3D theater, and tropical rain forest, all in one place! It will take you and your family on a spectacular journey of discovery as you explore our incredible world and the universe beyond.

Cherry Blossom Festival of Northern California

Bloomin' Fun for Everyone!

During two spring weekends, the streets of Japantown bloom with the sights, sounds, and tastes of Japanese culture. This unique celebration includes dancing, singing, martial arts demonstrations, traditional foods, and much more. The festival has been bringing the unique and colorful Japanese heritage to light for over 40 years.

Chinese Cultural Center

Chinese culture is everywhere in San Francisco, and it all comes together at the Chinese Cultural Center. Since 1965, the center has featured artists, exhibits, lectures, performances and more. Members can even search their family roots with their Genealogy Research Service.

Chop Suey

No one really knows the real truth about how it started, but legend has it that chop suey was invented by a Chinese restaurant worker in San Francisco. At the end of the day, he was allowed to eat any of the leftovers, so he chopped them all up, added some sauce, and named it chop suey. It was so good, the customers started asking for it, and before long, every Chinese restaurant in town had "Chop Suey" on their menu.

Chinatown

Take an awesome walking tour through the oldest Chinatown in North America. It's like stepping into another world, with pagoda-topped shops filled with cultural trinkets, street fairs, and even a Fortune Cookie factory. Don't be surprised if you find some pretty unusual stuff cooking up at the local food markets. Dare to try it?

City Hall

San Francisco City Hall is enormous! It's even taller than the U.S. Capitol Building in Washington, D.C. It's built in the Beaux-Arts style—that's just another word for "fancy-French." The earthquake of 1989 caused the big dome to move a whole 4 inches. After that, it was repaired, so now it's earthquake-proof!

CityPASS
That's the Ticket!

What's the secret to unlimited cable-car rides and half price on admission to some of San Francisco's best attractions? CityPASS! It's your ticket to great places like the Aquarium of the Bay, the California Academy of Sciences, and even a Blue & Gold Fleet Bay Cruise. All at a great discount the grownups will love! Check out all the details at www.citypass.com.

Coastal Trail

Get on your hiking boots and hit the trail. The Coastal Trail, that is! From San Francisco Bay to the historic Cliff House, the Coastal Trail is a 10.5-mile hike that covers some of the most spectacular natural and man-made sites in the country. Along the way you'll see the famous Golden Gate Bridge, Fort Point, the Presidio, the Sutro Gardens, and more. This hiking stretch is part of the California Coastal Trail, which is 1200 miles long and passes through 15 different counties.

Concord Coaches
Snail Mail of the 1800s

A team of horses with a stagecoach in tow was what San Franciscans might have called "snail mail" back in the mid 1800s. The famous Wells Fargo coaches were part of the Overland Mail Company that carried people and parcels to San Francisco at a whopping 5 miles an hour! The coaches were made in Concord, New Hampshire by Lewis Downing and Stephen Abbott.

Coit Tower
A Monument With a Veiw

High on Telegraph Hill in Pioneer Park is Coit Tower. It was built in 1933 as a tribute to San Francisco's firefighters (see page 30). The fantastic view of the Bay Bridge, the piers, and Downtown is well worth the 210-foot climb to the top. And be sure to browse the Depression-era murals on the ground-floor walls and the statue of Christopher Columbus.

Crissy Fields

Crissy Fields, in Presidio National Park, is a great place to stroll, bike, or rollerblade while taking in awesome views of the Golden Gate Bridge. With Marina Green on the east side and Fort Point on the west side, the area is very popular for picnicking, sail boarding, and checking out tons of natural beauty. It used to be an army base, but now it's an environmental paradise.

Cupid's Arrow
Taking Aim at the Heart of
San Francisco

Love is in the air at Rincon Park, on the Embarcadero, where this huge 60-foot-high sculpture called *Cupid's Span* seems partially sunk into the ground. Sculptors Claes Oldenburg and Coosje van Bruggen created it in 2002 as a symbol of love. They also said it had the shape of a sailing ship's bow. What does it remind *you* of?

Dahlia
Official
Flower of
San Francisco

Why is the Dahlia the official flower of San Francisco? Because so many of its qualities reflect what this great city is all about. Being able to thrive in most soil, it's strong and hearty, like the early pioneers. It also comes in many colors, which represents the variety of art and poetry found everywhere around the city. Just look around… it's easy to see why the Dahlia's beauty and strength is a symbol of the spirit of the people of San Francisco.

de Young Museum

The de Young Museum is an incredible building made of copper, stone, wood, and glass. It blends in perfectly with the natural surroundings of Golden Gate Park. Inside is a great collection of American, African, and Oceanic Art ready to be discovered. There are also artist demonstrations, programs, and special events that will bring out the artist in you!

Doggie Diner Sign
Long Live the Doggie!

This happy pup was created in 1966 as an advertising plan to sell hamburgers. He grinned at Doggie Diner patrons till the last one closed in 1986. Diana Scott and Joel Schechter of the Ocean Beach Historical Society thought it was important to save the very last doggie head. So, it was moved to 45th Avenue in 2005 and is now a landmark that welcomes all to Ocean Beach with a plaque that reads "Long Live the Doggie!"

Dragon
The Chinese Good Luck Charm

The Chinese New Year is celebrated in Chinatown with a nighttime parade that features a glowing dragon that's over 200 feet long! The dragon is called *Gum Lung* which means "Golden Dragon" and is a symbol of strength and goodness. It appears at the end of the parade to wish everyone peace, prosperity, and good luck for the coming year.

Dungeness Crab
A Tasty Treat!

If you love this scrumptious crustacean, you'll definitely want to be around for the start of San Francisco's crab season in November. The Dungeness Crab lives in the super-cold waters of the Pacific Ocean. It's a sweet and tasty delicacy that can be found in restaurants and at festivals throughout San Francisco, from the Fisherman's Wharf Crab Festival to the North Beach Crab Crawl and the Union Square Crab Fest. So crawl on over and enjoy!

Early Days Sculpture

The *Early Days* sculpture is part of the *Pioneer's Monument,* a tribute to San Francisco's early pioneers. It's in Alamo Square on Fulton Street. It was created by F.H. Happersberger in 1894, and has different parts—each representing an important period in Californian history. Incredibly, it survived the earthquake in 1906. Rumor has it that there is a time capsule buried deep beneath the monument.

Earthquake and Fire of 1906

On April 18, 1906, just after 5:00 o'clock in the morning, San Francisco was rocked by one of the most devastating earthquakes of all time. It ruptured the northernmost 296 miles of the San Andreas Fault, and the shaking was felt as far east as central Nevada. Many buildings collapsed and fires erupted, some lasting for four days. After the quake, the Army was called in to patrol streets and guard the U.S. Mint. Although many lost their lives, the people of San Francisco started the clean up and rebuilding almost immediately.

One hundred years later, astronomers at the University of California's Lick Observatory on Mount Hamilton took a trip back in time when they found what they thought might be original recordings of this great earthquake.

Embarcadero
Walk or Bike It

Take a bike ride along a wide boulevard called the Embarcadero and enjoy some great views of the bay. There are lots of interesting places to stop along the way. Get a bite to eat at the Ferry Building, check out the boats docked at Fisherman's Wharf, and see what people are catching as they fish along the piers. The route will take you all the way to Aquatic Park.

Escape from Alcatraz!
Ready, Set, Go!

You don't have to be a prisoner, but you do have to be in tip-top shape to take part in the Escape from Alcatraz Triathlon. The race takes place every summer and includes a mile and a half swim from Alcatraz Island to the shore, then an 18-mile bicycle race, and finally, an 8-mile foot race through Golden Gate National Recreation Area. Whew! Better start training.

Exploratorium
A World of Wonder

Have you ever wondered what your age would be on Mars? Or how a garden grows in Antarctica? The Exploratorium is a great place to find out. More than just a museum, it's a place to discover science, art, and how to use all of your senses to learn about our world. Learn to "see" using only your sense of touch in the *Tactile Dome*, a favorite exhibit that plunges you into total darkness! You can visit the Exploratorium at the Palace of Fine Arts on Lyon Street. And if you can't get there, you can always check out their way-cool interactive exhibits online at www.exploritorium.edu.

49ers
Super Bowl Champs

The San Francisco 49ers were named in honor of miners who rushed west for gold. The original owners saw a photograph on the side of a freight train that had a miner firing a pistol, and that's how they chose the name of their football team!

49-Mile Scenic Drive
Miles of Smiles Begin and End at City Hall

The 49-Mile Scenic Drive winds past some of the most beautiful areas of the city. You know you're on it if you see those blue and white seagull signs. The route meanders past places like the Palace of Fine Arts, Mission Dolores, and Fisherman's Wharf. It curls around the Presidio, sails along the crashing waves of Ocean Beach, and climbs Twin Peaks, where there's a fabulous view.

Ferry Building

It used to be a major transportation center back in 1898, but today, the Ferry Building is the place to be if great food is what floats your boat. Renovated in 2003, it now features boutique food shops, restaurants, and a popular weekly farmer's market. It's easy to spot along the waterfront, with its incredible 245-foot-tall clock tower.

Filbert Steps
What a Workout!

The Filbert Steps climb an incredibly steep cliff in three sections of stairwells that start at Sansome Street and rise all the way to Coit Tower. Along the way are cool, art deco buildings and spectacular gardens. You'll huff and puff, but at the top, the awesome view is well worth it.

First Transcontinental Telephone Call

It would be years before "speed dial," but back in 1915, the first transcontinental phone call was made between New York and San Francisco. Inventor Alexander Graham Bell was on the East Coast when he gave a shout to his colleague Thomas Watson who was over on the West Coast. When someone asked Mr. Bell to repeat his famous first words, "Mr. Watson, come here, I want you," Mr. Watson, who was miles away, answered, "It would take me a week now!"

Flag
Phoenix Rising

The phoenix of Greek mythology kept rising up from fire and ash over and over again. Maybe that's why the people of San Francisco have one on their flag. The city suffered several fires and earthquakes and has come back better than ever each time.

The motto beneath the phoenix *Oro en Paz—Fierro en Guerra* means "Gold in Peace, Iron in War."

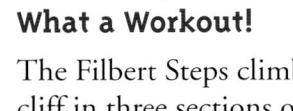

Fort Point
Still Keeping Watch

In the shadow of the Golden Gate Bridge, Fort Point has been keeping watch over San Francisco Bay for almost 150 years. Although it was built by the military to protect against attack during war time, the fort never actually fired a single shot in battle. Sometimes called "The Gibraltar of the West Coast," the building is an excellent example of American military masonry. Fort Point is now a National Historic Site.

Fortune Cookie
Try Your Luck!

This sweet Chinese treat filled with a little bit of wisdom was actually invented by the Japanese Hagiwara family at Golden Gate Park's Tea Garden. You can bite into one at the Golden Gate Fortune Cookie Factory in Chinatown. They've been making fortune cookies there by hand, the old fashioned way, since around 1909.

Ghirardelli Square
A Chocolate Lover's Dream

In 1852, Domingo Ghirardelli opened a general store in San Francisco and sold stuff like coffee, spices, and of course, chocolate, to gold-rush pioneer families. His old chocolate factory has since changed to a variety of shops and restaurants including the Ghirardelli Ice Cream and Chocolate Shop, where you can dig into a huge sundae and taste the best chocolates around. You can still see the original chocolate-making equipment in action.

Giants
World Series Champs!

The Giants began playing baseball in San Francisco back in 1957. In 1960, the famous Candlestick Park became their home and, for forty years, they played in all kinds of crazy weather like strong winds, freezing temperatures, and thick fog. In 2000, a new stadium, now called AT&T Park, gave the team a new start at a much more modern stadium that also has spectacular waterfront views.

Gold Rush

"Gold from the American River!"

The California Gold Rush started in 1848, when James Wilson Marshall found a few flakes of gold while building a sawmill for John Sutter. Once San Francisco newspapers reported that gold had been discovered along the banks of the American River, people came in droves from all over, leaving behind their jobs, farms, and families to seek their fortune. "Gold fever" was running rampant, and populations boomed as prospectors were pulling about $50,000 worth of gold from the mines every day. They were called '49ers' because that was the year they decided to risk it all, and head west by the thousands, in an attempt to strike it rich.

Goddess of Democracy

The *Goddess of Democracy* is a bronze statue that is dedicated to everyone who works hard for human rights and democracy. It was designed by sculptor Thomas Marsh in 1989 and was dedicated on June 4, 1994 in Portsmouth Square Park in Chinatown. Five anonymous Chinese artists helped Marsh in creating the final statue. It's a 1/4-scale re-creation of the original *Goddess of Liberty* that was created by Chinese students during the movement for democracy in Beijing, China.

Golden Gate Bridge
They Said It Couldn't Be Done

In 1916, engineer Joseph Strauss came up with a design for the Golden Gate Bridge. The structure was sound, but the design was pretty ugly. In fact, it was so ugly, that two architects, Irving and Gertrude Morrow, decided to step in and create a new design, and it was finally opened to traffic in 1937. Its deck sits 220 feet above water and the tallest tower is 746 feet above the water. The bridge spans 1.7 miles across San Francisco Bay's entrance, which was named *Chrysopylae*, which means "golden gate," by Captain John C. Fremont in 1846.

Golden Gate National Recreation Area

On either side of the Golden Gate Bridge is the Golden Gate National Recreation Area. It's the largest urban national park in the world, with over 76,500 acres that includes 28 miles of coastline. The area comprises Fort Point National Historic Site, Muir Woods National Monument, Alcatraz Island, and the Presidio. It's surprising to find so much wildlife, like hawks and deer, so close to a big city.

The Haight
Far out, Man!

During the mid 1960s, the corner of Haight and Ashbury Streets, known as The Haight, was a place where hippies hung out to find 'peace and love.' It was the flower-power era and great rock bands like the Grateful Dead were really inspired by this neighborhood. Never heard of them? Ask your parents!

Hallidie Plaza

Hallidie Plaza is an area at the foot of Powell Street where the cable cars turn around. It's named after Andrew Smith Hallidie who was the inventor of the cable car (see page 10). The Plaza is action packed with street vendors, performing artists, and tons of tourists on their urban hike. You can still see the old-fashioned, three-torched street light from 1917.

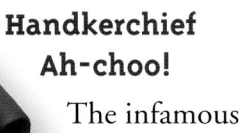

Handkerchief
Ah-choo!

The infamous stagecoach robber, Black Bart, accidentally left behind a clue for detectives—his handkerchief—which led to his arrest in San Francisco in 1883. During his reckless crime spree, he robbed 28 stagecoaches in Northern California between 1875-1883.

ANDREW S. HALLIDIE
1836 - 1900

THIS PLAZA IS DEDICATED TO ANDREW S. HALLIDIE, DEVELOPER OF THE CABLE STREET RAILWAY IN 1873. HIS INGENUITY GAVE SAN FRANCISCO THE CABLE CAR, MEMORIALIZED IN SONG, DECLARED A NATIONAL LANDMARK AND FOREVER LOVED BY THE PEOPLE.

Haunted
Strange Happenings

Flickering lights, doors opening and closing, and footsteps in the night—there's been a lot of unexplained weirdness going on here. This creepy looking tower is part of the San Francisco Art Institute, but it used to be a burial ground. During renovations in 1968 there were so many strange and odd accidents that construction workers were too scared to work there. Maybe the ghosts didn't like all the noise, but for whatever reason, the tower is now closed.

Herschell-Spillman Carousel
Ride the Colorful Critters of Old

Galloping ostriches, cantering camels, leaping lions, and frolicking frogs—this is not your typical carousel. A true work of art, this classic wooden carousel in Golden Gate Park was built in 1914. Along with jumping horses, other colorful critters that bob to the beat of the band organ include a tiger, giraffe, stork, deer, goat, and dragon. Fanciful cats, dogs, roosters, zebras, mules, and pigs round out the friendly herd.

Hyde Street Pier

Before the Golden Gate and Oakland Bay bridges were built, the way to get around was by ferry. Hyde Street Pier was the main automobile ferry terminal. The pier, where famous ships like the *Balclutha* anchor, is part of the San Francisco Maritime National Historical Park.

Immigration Station
One Hundred Years Old

On January 21, 1910, over one hundred years ago, the immigration station on Angel Island opened. This is where over 500,000 immigrants, mostly Asian, were processed into the United States. After a fire in 1940, the station was closed. Since then the buildings have been restored, and Angel Island is now a national park.

Infinite Mirror Maze
Pure, Mind-boggling Fun!

Magowan's Infinite Mirror Maze at Fisherman's Wharf is a kaleidoscope of mirrors, lights, and sound that's a blast from the minute you enter. Feel your way along as you find the path among halls that really seem to go on forever. It's a dizzying effect that will take you by surprise with every turn.

International Orange
More Than a Matter of Taste

Have you ever wondered about the color of the Golden Gate Bridge? It's called International Orange. This deep red hue is used for safety reasons—it makes things really stand out in their environment. With all the heavy fog here, it makes a lot of sense to use this color. As part of the upkeep, bridge workers continually slather it with about 10,000 gallons of paint a year.

Japanese Peace Pagoda

It looks like some weird kind of alien space ship, but actually, this 100-foot-tall monument is a symbol of peace between Japan and America. Designed by Japanese architect Yoshiro Taniguchi, it's part of the five-acre Japan Center complex and was given to the people of San Francisco by the people of Osaka, Japan.

Japanese Tea Garden
It's Everybody's Cup of Tea

It's one of the oldest public Japanese gardens in the country and one of the most popular attractions in San Francisco. Makoto Hagiwara, a Japanese immigrant, designed most of the garden spaces in 1894, for the World's Fair. He was caretaker up until World War II. Stroll though the lush grounds and see native Japanese plants, beautiful monuments, and bridges. Take a peaceful break at the tea house that overlooks the garden waters and enjoy authentic teas and snacks.

Japantown
Culture and Customs at Every Turn.

Asian families settled in this area after the big earthquake of 1906. Along with their houses, they opened shops, hotels, and restaurants in what is now called Japantown. One of the most famous events in Japantown is the Cherry Blossom Festival (see page 11). For two weekends in April, there is a huge celebration of Japanese-American heritage. The streets are filled with traditional music, wonderful aromas, and costumed dancers. The highlight is a two-hour parade with musicians, samurai floats, and ladies dressed in colorful kimonos.

Kayaking For Baseballs?

A lot of kayaking goes on in McCovey Cove outside of AT&T Park. Whether it's a day game or a night game, paddlers brave the frigid waters and eagerly wait to chase after the next home run or "splash-hit." Fielding balls from the Bay has become a new tradition that sometimes lasts up to 5 hours if you include batting practice! It makes for a long day, but if you decide to rent a kayak and head out to McCovey Cove, don't forget your glove!

Knickerbocker Engine Company No. 5

This little volunteer firehouse, established in 1850, comes with an unusual story. When a fire broke out in 1858 atop Telegraph Hill, the engine was having a hard time getting up the hill. Little girls were

not expected to be so brave back in those days, but on her way back from school, young Lillie Hitchcock ran to help and called for others to pull on the ropes to get the engine uphill. Everyone pulled hard and the engine was the first to put water on the fire. After that, it was hard to keep Lillie away from the excitement once an alarm was sounded. She later became an honorary member of the Knickerbocker Company. Even after she married Howard Coit, she still remained dedicated to the firehouse and to the city of San Francisco. When she died, a huge monument, Coit Tower (see page 14) was built in her honor. It stands 180 feet high up on Telegraph Hill, where her story had started.

Knothole Gang

There's a great way to watch the World Series Champs, Giants, for free! Just join the "knothole gang" along the Port Walk behind right field. There are cut-out portholes that let you take in all the action at the ballpark. It's a good idea to watch only an inning or two at a time so that others can sneak a peek, too!

Koret Children's Quarter
A Kid-friendly Zone in Golden Gate Park!

The Koret Children's Quarter is one of the best playgrounds around, with huge concrete slides, miniature space ships, and walls and webs to climb. It's a one-of-a-kind hot spot for kids, with sand areas, grass areas, and soft rubber matting areas for wide-open fun. It's believed to be the first playground in America, originating back in 1887. With a charming, historic carousel nearby, this sprawling park is a great time for all.

Legion of Honor
Art for the Heart, Mind, and Soul

Together with the de Young Museum in Golden Gate Park, the Legion of Honor in Lincoln Park is part of the Fine Arts Museums of San Francisco. It's home to the famous sculpture, *The Thinker* (see page 51).

Lincoln Golf Course

It was once a cemetery, but in 1909 the city decided to use the land for a more lively use. The cemetery was respectfully moved and Lincoln Golf Course first opened with 9 holes in 1909. By 1917, it had a full 18 holes. The beautiful ocean views will make you forget you're playing on what once was a burial ground.

Lions
Sea Lions, That Is!

These huge pinnipeds (mammals with flipper-like limbs) can weigh up to half a ton, and boy, can they bark! Sea lions hang out on Pier 39, attracting lots of attention. There have been up to 1,139 of these blubbery brutes reported at one time! Be sure to visit the Marine Mammal Center with all your questions about these playful creatures.

Lombard Street
Whoa, Nelly!

Hold on tight for a wild ride! Just a few blocks uphill from Ghirardelli Square is a famous street known as the "crookedest street." Lombard Street is made up of eight hard turns on a 40-degree slope. On foot, you can use the sidewalks to watch the nervous drivers white-knuckle it through the crazy twists and turns.

Lombard Street is called the "crookedest street" but it's really not. With all it's zigs and zags, Vermont Avenue between 22nd and 23rd is actually more crooked!

Maritime National Park
Seafaring History

The Maritime National Park, located in the Fisherman's Wharf neighborhood, is where National Historic Landmark vessels like the 1886 square-rigger *Balclutha*, and the 1890 steam ferryboat *Eureka* are docked. You can see other ships, too, like the graceful lines of the schooners *Alma*, *C.A. Thayer*, and *Wapama*—they'll leave you breathless! You can even go aboard the steam tug *Hercules* for an unforgettable adventure, and don't forget to visit the really cool Maritime Store!

Martin Luther King, Jr. Memorial

In Yerba Buena Gardens, behind a dramatically lit waterfall that is 50 feet high and 20 feet wide, is a memorial that is dedicated to Dr. King's vision of equality. Twelve glass panels set in granite are inscribed with the inspirational words of Dr. King that are translated into 13 different languages. The memorial also includes photographs from the civil rights movement. This very impressive tribute is the second largest King Memorial in the country.

Meiggs' Wharf
What's in a name?

Meiggs' Wharf was the original name for what is now the famous Fisherman's Wharf. It was first completed in 1853 for lumber trade use by Henry Meiggs, a scheming businessman with a bad reputation. It was also a great spot for fishermen to dock their boats. Meiggs was eventually run out of town by his creditors and the name changed to Fisherman's Wharf at the turn of the century.

Mission Dolores

Completed in 1791, Mission San Francisco de Asisi, (now Mission Dolores), has great historic and architectural significance, being the oldest building in the city. It has seen the likes of the California Goldrush and the 1906 earthquake. The Mission Cemetery is the resting place of many of the first Californians like Wyatt Earp and famous Californians like Joe DiMaggio.

Metreon

The Metreon is four floors, some 350,000 square feet, of great entertainment. The 15-movie-screen theater includes a cool IMAX theater, and the gaming arcade will keep kids of all ages immersed for hours. The *Walk of Game* is an added attraction that spotlights the movers and shakers of the video game industry. But perhaps one of the Metreon's best features can be found outdoors with the great view of the Yerba Buena Gardens and Museum of Modern Art.

Morrison Planetarium
Take a Trip Across
the Universe

For the ultimate interplanetary experience, rocket on over to the Morrison Planetarium. The tilted theater, sloped at a 30-degree angle, and stadium-like seating allow you to view amazing light shows that cover the entire dome. The digital projection system takes you skyward on a trip flying through the stars. It's an astral adventure of a lifetime.

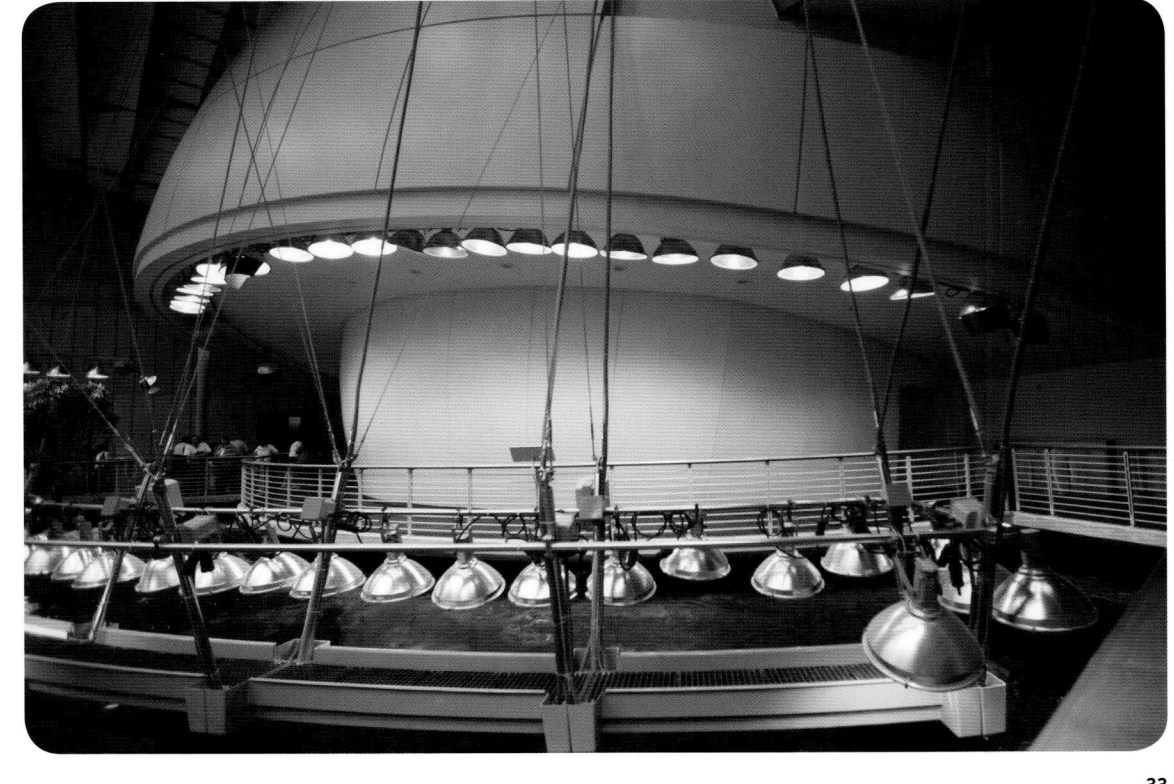

Muir Woods
One Thousand Year Old Trees!

The giant coast redwoods of Muir Woods are the tallest living things on the planet at over 386 feet, and some of them are 1,000 years old! This ancient redwood forest is a 560-acre park with six miles of paved trails for easy strolling. Longer hiking trails are unpaved. The forest floor is damp and cool, forcing the enormous trees to reach high for all the warm sun they can get.

Museums on Wheels
Riding Through History

This is one of the few places in the world where you can ride vintage railway cars from the good old days. These restored streetcars are called "museums on wheels" and are part of the San Francisco Railway Museum experience. Before you ride the cars, be sure to visit the museum to get the inside scoop on San Francisco's rail transit history.

MARKET STREET RAILWAY'S
SAN FRANCISCO
— RAILWAY —
MUSEUM
AND
GIFT SHOP
77 STEUART ST

National AIDS Memorial Grove

A living memorial of flower beds and shady trees in San Francisco's Golden Gate Park, the National AIDS Memorial Grove is a comforting place for all who have been touched by AIDS (acquired immune deficiency syndrome). It was officially designated a National Memorial in 1996. It is a special place to heal, to remember, and to learn about this sad epidemic.

The AIDS Memorial Quilt is the largest piece of folk art in the world. It has over 46,000 panels and weighs about 54 tons!

That's the same as a dozen full-grown elephants! Each 3-foot by 6-foot panel is hand made and celebrates the life of someone who has died of AIDS. Activist Cleve Jones thought of the idea for the NAMES Project Memorial Quilt in 1985 when people wrote the names of lost loved ones on signs and taped them to a building. He thought it looked a lot like a big patchwork quilt!

National Liberty Ship Memorial

Longer than a football field, Liberty Ships were gigantic cargo ships that hauled tons of troops and supplies across miles of ocean during World War II. At the National Liberty Ship Memorial, you can tour the S.S. *Jeremiah O'Brien*—a real Liberty Ship. You can even bring your sleeping bag for a cool overnight adventure.

Nob Hill
A Very Swanky Neighborhood

Rich San Franciscans have been living high on the hog up on Nob Hill since the Gold Rush days. People who made their fortunes in the early days built grand mansions that overlooked the city below. Today, in place of fancy homes are big, luxury hotels like the Farimont, upscale boutiques, and beautiful city landmarks like the *Fountain of the Tortoises*.

North Beach
Viva Italiano!

If you love Italian food, then follow the Barbary Coast Trail to the North Beach district. It's San Francisco's Little Italy where the aroma of Italian restaurants and bakeries is simply irresistible. In June the North Beach Festival features food, music, and animal blessings, as well as *Arte di Gesso* (Italian street chalk art).

"Oh, Say, Can You See?"

Do you know who wrote *The Star-Spangled Banner*? It was Francis Scott Key, the son of a Revolutionary officer. He was inspired in 1814, after he witnessed a battle and saw the stars and stripes of the America flag still waving in the morning when it was all over. He actually wrote the poem on the back of a letter he had in his pocket! This impressive monument to Key is in Golden Gate Park.

Ohlone Indians

The Ohlone Indians lived around the San Francisco and Monterey Bay areas. Once called *Costanoans* (meaning people of the coast), they were particularly known for their crafts, and wove baskets with intricate designs. Some would take months to make. The Ohlone made houses out of willows that only lasted one season, and the entrances were so small, they had to crawl though them to get in!

Old Del Monte Cannery
A Building With a Fruity Past

The Cannery was founded in 1907 by the California Fruit Company, which later became Del Monte. It survived the great earthquake and the canning of fruits and veggies continued on until 1937. It was once the most productive peach canning operation in the world! Today, the building has been restored and is an historic landmark with three floors of shops and restaurants.

Old United States Mint

During the Gold Rush days in 1852, there was so much gold that the government opened up a small building where they could turn it into coins. By 1854, they needed even more space and the larger U.S. Mint was built. It was the only building operating after the big earthquake and fire. Although it doesn't make the kind of coins you'd find in your pocket anymore, it still makes beautiful silver proof coin sets.

Orchids

This rare beauty, and many more like it, can be found at the Conservatory of Flowers. The oldest wood and glass conservatory in North America, it's a living museum of exotic plants and tropical flowers that's a real celebration for the senses. On the first Tuesday of every month, admission to the Conservatory is free!

Panama-Pacific International Exposition

When the Panama Canal was finished in 1914, the city of San Francisco decided to celebrate with a huge World's Fair. Exhibits included a steam locomotive and the actual Liberty Bell. And even though it probably didn't sound much different from the Atlantic Ocean, a telephone line was set up so that the people on the East Coast could hear what the Pacific Ocean sounded like! The only building left from the 1915 Exposition is the renovated Palace of Fine Arts—it's now a great place to see your favorite performers.

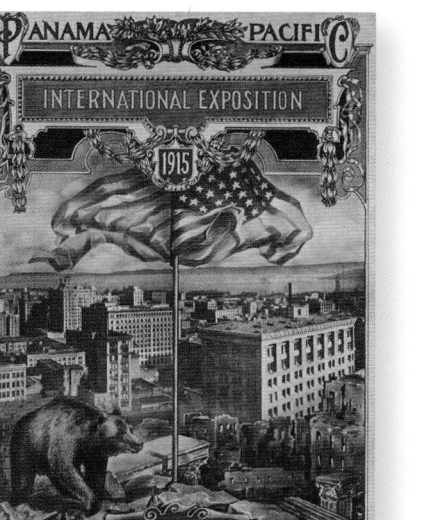

Peddle Boats
Are You a Peddler or a Paddler?

Either way, you'll have a great day out on the water at Stow Lake, the biggest lake in Golden Gate Park. Right in the middle of the lake is an island called Strawberry Hill. You can get to it by boat or by bridge, but which ever way you choose, be sure not to miss the beautiful Huntington Falls cascading down Strawberry Hill and into the lake.

Philippine Coral Reef
Under Water Wonders

Did you know that the reef systems in the Philippines have more varieties of corals and fishes than any other place on the planet? Maybe that's why the California Academy of Sciences chose to feature one in an exhibit that is one of the world's deepest living coral reef displays in the world. The 25-foot-tall tank holds a whopping 212,000 gallons of water, where you can see not only hard and soft corals, but also rays, sharks, and over 2,000 vibrantly colored fishes.

Pier 39

If you like to shop, eat, or just enjoy the beautiful picturesque bay with its quaint fishing boats and views of the Golden Gate Bridge, then Pier 39 is the place to be. Check out the sea lions that lounge on the docks or go for a high-speed adventure on a wild RocketBoat ride. Arcades, street performers, sailing charters—there's so much to do and see.

Point Bonita Lighthouse

Oops! Point Bonita's first lighthouse was built on its highest hill, but it was not much use to mariners because, at that height, it was in a fogbank most of the time! The second attempt was much better with the lighthouse sitting atop a lower rocky crag. Since then, the Point Bonita Lighthouse has had a long history of guiding ships through stormy waters and thick fog.

Pony Express
Giddy Up!

Over one hundred and fifty years ago, riders saddled up to bring news and mail from West to East. The Pony Express took only 10 days to deliver a letter, which was pretty fast back then. Express riders risked searing heat, snowstorms, and Indian attacks all along the 1,966-mile ride from San Francisco to Missouri. Much to their relief, they were phased out once the telegraph first crossed the continent. These plaques can be found on Clay Street where Chinatown meets the Financial District, which is where the headquarters was located for the Pony Express.

Powell Street Cable Car Turntable

While bigger cable cars can be operated from either end with the flick of a switch, the Powell-Hyde and Powell-Mason lines use smaller cars that only operate from one end. So what does the gripman do when they get to the end of the line? A man-powered turntable spins the cars around! Turntables are located at Taylor and Bay, and at the other end of the line at Fisherman's Wharf. They're quite a sight to see.

Presidio

The Presidio is a beautiful area just south of the Golden Gate Bridge that has forests, marshes, and beaches, all with spectacular views. It was first owned by Spain, then by Mexico, and finally, the United States. There are more than 500 historic buildings to discover, and even an historic airfield.

Queasy

You might think twice about walking across the Golden Gate Bridge if the thought of being 220 feet above the water makes you a little queasy. But if you're okay with that, then grab your windbreaker and prepare to be blown away by a refreshing hike across San Francisco's most famous landmark.

GOLDEN GATE BRIDGE
MAIN SPAN
4200 FEET

LENGTH OF ONE CABLE .... 7650 FT. (2331.7m)
DIAMETER OF ONE CABLE .... 36⅜ IN. (92.4 cm)
WIRES IN EACH CABLE 27,572
TOTAL WIRE USED ... 80,000 MILES (128,748 km)
WEIGHT OF CABLE (SUSPENDERS & ACCESSORIES) 24,500 TONS (22,226 m.tons)

Cable Contractor: John A. Roebling's Sons Co.
Trenton & Roebling, New Jersey

Queen Wilhelmina Tulip Garden

If you tiptoe through the Queen Wilhelmina Tulip Garden in Golden Gate Park, you'll come across a remarkable Dutch Windmill. It was built in 1902 and was originally used for park irrigation. It stands 75-feet high and has a span of 102 feet.

Questions and Answers

Turn the page upside down to see the answers!

- Why is San Francisco so much fun to walk?
- Besides San Francisco, who has the largest Chinese community in the world?
- Why is the Golden Gate Bridge golden?
- What happens to the Golden Gate Bridge during an earthquake?
- What is the nickname for San Francisco?

- Because it's built on 43 hills.
- Why, China, of course!
- It's International Orange, a color that makes it easy to see in the fog.
- The bridge is built to sway 27 feet in an earthquake.
- It's called "The City by the Bay."

Rainforest
California Academy of
Sciences Exhibit

This entire rainforest is inside a 90-foot glass bubble! Ride a glass elevator down from the treetops to below the flooded forest floor, where you can walk through an acrylic tunnel and see what's swimming above you. Did you know that almost one quarter of the world's medicines come from plants in rainforests? Maybe that's why they call them the "pharmacies of the earth."

Ripley's Believe It Or Not®

Shrunken heads? A space shuttle made out of matchsticks? If you're into the surreal, then a visit to Ripley's is a must. Ripley's has been feeding curious minds since the 1933 Chicago World's Fair. The 30 museums around the world host 12 million visitors a year. At the newly renovated San Francisco museum at Fisherman's Wharf, there are lots of strange, cool exhibits— even a candy factory where you can mix and match you favorite sweets. You're sure to learn something new and interesting in this "world of the weird."

RocketBoat
A Wet and Wild Ride!

Jump onto a RocketBoat at Pier 39 for a thirty-minute thrill ride around San Francisco Bay. These boats are crazy fast. Powerful engines rev at top speeds, propelling these fiery-red bullets through the waves, twisting and turning to the beat of high-energy rock music. It's a blast and you'll never want it to end!

Rose Window At Grace Cathedral

Over three thousand pieces of colorful glass make up this incredible geometric work of art. Sunlight filters through and paints the enormous interior with rainbows or sparkling light. Grace Church was founded in 1849, during the Gold Rush, and this cathedral was built in 1964. A lot of people visit to take in the colorful stained glass artwork, listen to the 44-bell carillon, and to walk the peaceful paths of the indoor and outdoor labyrinths.

Ross Alley
San Francisco's Oldest Alley

You just might recognize this alleyway from movies like *Indian Jones and the Temple of Doom*, or *Karate Kid II*. It's a back street with a checkered past, but today you can see a lot of amazing attractions here like these lifelike murals that show everyday Chinese-American life and the Golden Gate Fortune Cookie Factory where you can watch cookies being made by hand.

Sailors
Riding the Breezy Bay

Wind and water are just the right combination when you're looking for fun on the Bay. With all the beautiful, windy weather in San Francisco, it's no wonder that sailors flock here for boating, windsurfing, and kiteboarding.

San Francisco Botanical Garden at Strybing Arboretum

Imagine! Fifty-five acres of trees, flowers, and shrubs from all over the world. That's what you'll find at the Arboretum in Golden Gate Park. Free to the pubic, this birdwatcher's paradise is actually made up of many different kinds of gardens and has seven ponds where the waterfowl love to hang out. Helene Strybing funded the garden and it was named in memory of her husband, Christian M. Strybing.

San Francisco Fire Department Museum

From vintage firehouses to horse-drawn engines to modern fireboats, this museum is a great place to uncover the history of the "Guardians of the City." Learn about the Great Fires of San Francisco and how these brave firefighters meet the challenges of all this hilly terrain. The museum is open Thursday through Sunday from 1:00 to 4:00.

San Francisco Museum of Modern Art

Discover your inner artist at San Francisco Museum of Modern Art. Explore, create, and get inspired with guided tours, activities, and special family-friendly programs. Check out the museum's way cool online ArtScope, a fun, interactive tool you can use to lose yourself in over 5,000 works of art in their collection.

Sightseeing Tours

Looking for a fun way to see the city? You can check out all of the most popular attractions from an open-top, double-decker bus; or how about a boat ride around the Bay, or a cool GPS Go Car tour. And if you're looking for something really different, you can even tour the city by Segway!

Shanghai

"Aunt Bessie *shanghai*-ed us to weed the garden!" Have you ever wondered where the word *shanghai* came from? Well, long ago, there was a huge demand for deck hands on ships heading from San Francisco to the port of Shanghai, China. So when men were scarce and work was plenty, a lot of unfortunate souls were kidnapped and forced to work once out at sea. That's where the term *shanghai* came from. Boy, it must have been really hard to find good help in those days!

Shipwrecks

Did you know that part of San Francisco is built right on top of a bunch of shipwrecks? Some have even been found underground in the Jackson Square Historic District. There were no automobiles or railroads to San Francisco during the Gold Rush, so the best way to get to the gold was from its port. People rushed to get here and whole crews just abandoned their ships! San Francisco was left with an estimated 600 shipwrecks!

"The Stick"
Candlestick Park: Home of the 49ers

Candlestick Park first opened in 1960. Fans chose that name because it sits right at the top of Candlestick Point. It was built in the shape of a boomerang to shield out the chilly winds from the water, but that really didn't' work so well— the winds still howl here. No matter—49ers fans are a hearty bunch. So hearty, in fact that they put away about 150,000 hot dogs and sausages, and over 130,000 sodas from the concession stands every season! The 49ers mascot is named "Sourdough Sam." Read the first entry on this page to find out why.

Surfing

Most people think of Southern California when they think of surfing, but San Francisco has some pretty fantastic surfing, too, especially off of Fort Point, with the majestic Golden Gate Bridge as the backdrop. The best waves roll in during the fall when big Alaskan swells move in and the looming summer fog clears out.

Sourdough Bread
"The Mother Dough"

San Francisco has long been famous for its delicious sourdough bread. Miners during the Gold Rush days couldn't get enough of this new and tasty bread. Every morning, they flocked to the shop of the Boudin family, master bakers from France, who perfected the recipe with the special dough they called the "Mother Dough." Strangely enough, the dough was also used to tan animal hides by rubbing it into the skin.

Starfleet Command Headquarters
Are You a Trekie?

If you are, then you may already know that San Francisco is the home of Starfleet Command Headquarters. Star Trek movies have shown the headquarters as being located at Fort Baker, across from the Golden Gate Bridge, and, according to StarTrek.com, the famous Starfleet ship *Enterprise* was built on San Francisco's Mare Island in the year 2245. As the Vulcans say, "live long and prosper!"

Tankers

A huge tanker ship carefully slips under the Golden Gate Bridge, and from this angle, it looks like it might be a tight fit! These gigantic vessels often depend on the services of much smaller tugboats to help guide them in and out of port.

Telegraph Hill
Who Goes There?

This was originally a signal tower for ships heading into the Golden Gate. A watchman on the hill could tell where the ships were from by their flags, and then he would telegraph that information to its townspeople. The plaque at the Christopher Columbus statue marks the spot where the watchman stood.

The Thinker

This famous sculpture, *The Thinker*, by August Rodin is part of the huge collection of art you can find at the Legion of Honor Museum. Nobody really knows for sure, but maybe he's thinking about all the other great things to see here, like the magnificent Skinner Pipe Organ, or the Book of Gold. Or it could be he's just wondering when your next visit will be!

Tower of Jewels
Sparkling Architecture

At over 400 feet tall, as high as many of San Francisco's hills, the Tower of Jewels was the crowning glory of the 1915 World's Fair (see page 38). The building was decorated with more than 120,000 "jewels" from Bohemia called Novagems. Even though they were only just colorful cut glass, the "gems" bedazzled the tower anyway.

Transamerica Pyramid Center

A lot of San Franciscans didn't like this new, triangle-shaped building at first. But, after a while, it started to grow on them, and now, this amazing, 853-foot-high pyramid with its pointy spire, has become an icon. Smart-thinking architect William Pereira designed it to move with earthquake tremors.

Treasure Island

A huge chunk of land was dredged up from the Bay in 1937 to form Treasure Island for the Golden Gate International Exposition of 1939. It was supposed to be used as an airport, but when WWII started, it was used as a Naval base instead. You can still visit Treasure Island Museum in the horseshoe-shaped administration building, but call ahead—hours are limited.

Twin Peaks
360-degree Views!

Hike through lush green forests to an elevation of over 900 feet to enjoy sweeping panoramic views of the city and the bay. These two identical hills are located right in the middle of the city. The lower portion is dotted with colorful houses, while the upper portion is an undeveloped nature preserve where, on a clear day, you just might be lucky enough to spot a redtailed hawk. But dress warmly and bring some hot chocolate. It can be chilly up there!

United Nations Plaza

Before the United Nations was moved to New York, it was here in San Francisco. This statue at Union Plaza is of Venezuelan military hero, Simón Bolívar, who helped to liberate many South American nations. It was a gift from the people of Venezuela.

USS Pampanito

If you're anywhere near Pier 45, be sure to check out the real WWII submarine that's moored there. The USS *Pampanito* is one of the most popular historic vessels in the country and gets more than 100,000 visitors a year. You can take a tour, but be careful if you're claustrophobic, the quarters can be pretty cramped!

Venetian Carousel
On Pier 39

Have you ever seen a double-decker carousel like this one? It's a work of art from Italy, with 32 hand-carved, mythical animals, and brightly painted scenes of San Francisco. No matter which critter you choose to ride, you'll be glad to learn that all the proceeds from ticket fares go directly to the Marine Mammal Center.

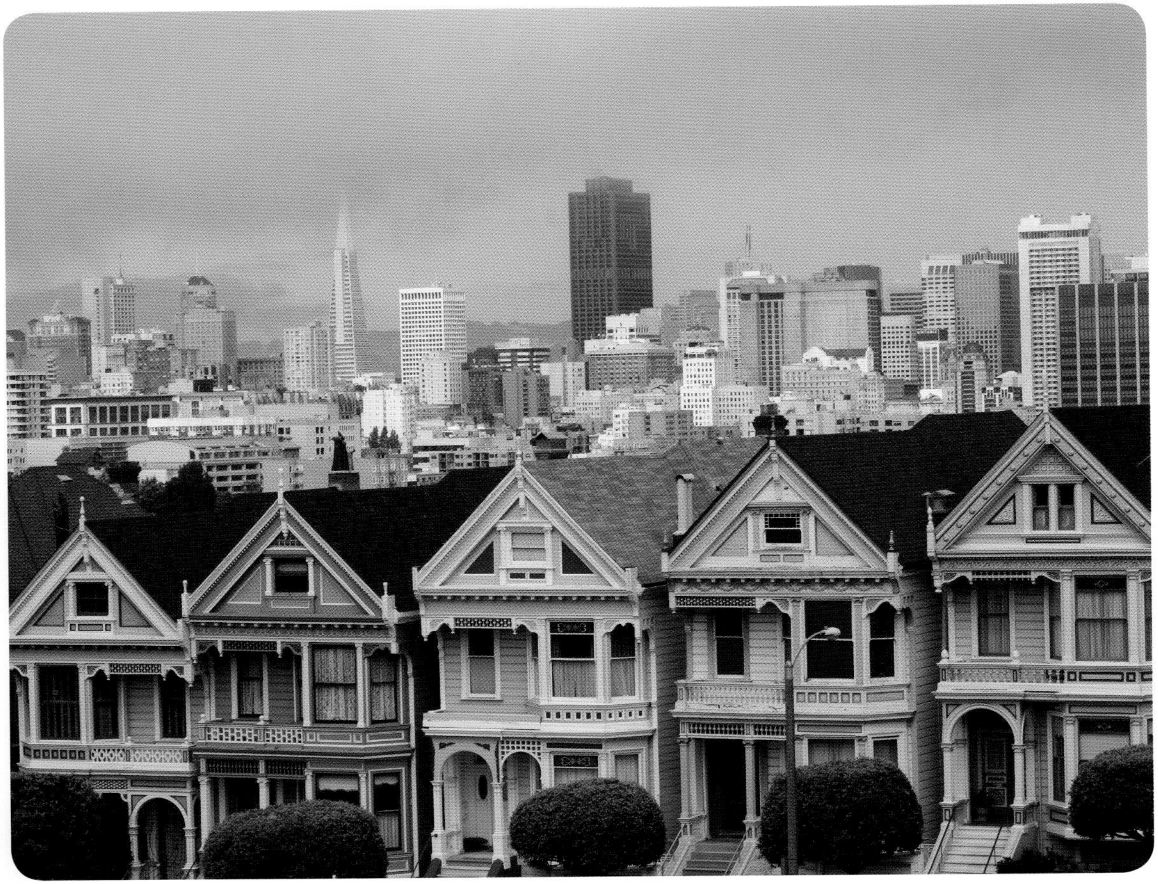

Walt Disney Family Museum

There was never a man who was more dedicated to fun and imagination than Walt Disney. From the humble beginnings of the first Mickey Mouse cartoon, *Steamboat Willie*, to the mega theme parks, you can find out all about the magic that started inside the mind of this incredible innovator. The museum is located in the Presidio of San Francisco.

Victorian Mansions
San Francisco's Painted Ladies

Victorian-style mansions are found throughout the city's neighborhoods. Most of these ornate buildings were home to those who made a lot of money in mining back in the Gold Rush days. If you've ever watched the TV show, *Full House*, you would have seen a "painted lady" in the opening credits. That's what multi-colored Victorian houses are called. You can find rows of these boldly painted homes all around the city of San Francisco. Sometimes known as "Postcard Row," the houses across from Alamo Square Park are a famous group of painted ladies. They have appeared on post cards and in ads, movies, and on TV shows.

Washington Square Park

It's the perfect community meeting spot for strolling, playing Frisbee, or taking in an outdoor movie. Located in the Italian North Beach neighborhood, this park is a wide-open oasis in a busy city. The impressive Coit Tower and this statue in the square both honor San Francisco's fire fighters (see pages 14 and 30).

Wax Museum
At Fisherman's Wharf

Where can you see Brad Pitt, Angelina Jolie, Yao Ming, and Tiger Woods all in the same place? They're all here at one of the largest wax museums in the world. There are over 200 personalities, including your favorite sports stars, military heroes, and creepy villains. Freddy Kruger and Vincent Price will greet you in the *Chamber of Horrors* exhibit where you're certain to be freaked out by the Head Crusher and other terrifying devices used in the Middle Ages.

Weird Weather
Got Fog?

Billowing blankets of cottony clouds, the "City by the Bay" is famous for fog. San Franciscans never tire of this majestic natural phenomenon that rolls in during the summer months. Many poets have been inspired by the fog's quiet beauty and by the muffled low tones of the foghorns.

Wells Fargo History Museum

Henry Wells and William Fargo first provided banking and express coach services during the Gold Rush days. The coaches (see page 14) were pulled by a team of six horses guided by skilled drivers. At the Wells Fargo History Museum, you can see banking artifacts, as well as real gold rush mining tools. You can even take a ride on a virtual stagecoach.

Wild Parrots!

What started out as a few house pets that flew the coop is now a huge, brightly colored, screeching colony. These feathered friends of South America have come to be beloved by city residents on Telegraph Hill. There's even a book about them called *The Wild Parrots of Telegraph Hill.* Pick it up for a truly heart-warming story.

X-braces
Quake-proof Engineering

Since the Oakland Bay Bridge is right between the San Andreas Faultline and the Hayward Fault Zone, it makes sense that engineers designed it to be quakeproof. X-braces and tension cables are all part of a dynamic design that help resist the forces of earthquake tremors.

Yerba Buena

The Spaniards first discovered California in the 1500s, but it took another 200 years before they would find this beautiful coastal area, since it was so well hidden by thick fog. The small village of Yerba Buena was established in 1839 and was named for the trailing vines of white wild flowers that are still found on Alcatraz Island. Yerba Buena means "good herb" in Spanish. The Americans renamed it San Francisco in 1839, after the Mexican war.

Yerba Buena Children's Gardens

Yerba Buena Gardens has a special place just for kids. Boys and girls have 130,000 square feet to discover, including a sand circle, a play stream, and a 25-foot slide. There's a labyrinth of hedges to get lost in, and a fully restored, hand-carved Zeum Carousel from 1906.

Zeum
Digital Fun!

Did you ever want to make your own digital cartoon? Or star in your own music video? Kids can do this and more at Zeum: San Francisco's Children's Museum. This is a cool, hands-on, multimedia arts and technology experience for kids of all ages. Paint with light, create digital art, or make your own stop-action claymation movie. At Zeum, let your imagination run wild!

Zoo

If you love animals, a trip to the San Francisco Zoo is a must for you. Lemurs from Madagascar, Australian wallaroos, Siberian tigers, and African lions are some of the more than 930 animals you'll find there. Giraffes, gorillas, zebras, and everybody's favorite, penguins, are waiting to greet you. Spread out over 100 acres, animals and visitors have been coming together at the San Francisco Zoo since 1929.

Index

My Trip to San Francisco

Date:

Stuff we did: